ESPRESSO

CULTURE & CUISINE

BY

KARL PETZKE AND

SARA SLAVIN

Photography: Karl Petzke

Art Direction / Styling: Sara Slavin

Text: Carolyn Miller

Design: Jennifer Morla

Food: Sandra Cook

CHRONICLE BOOKS

SAN FRANCISCO

Library of Congress Cataloging-in-

Publication data: Slavin, Sara.

Espresso: culture & cuisine/ by

Karl Petzke & Sara Slavin .

p. cm.

1. Espresso. I. Petzke, Karl. II. Title.

TX817.C6S57 1994

641.6'373—dc20   93-25397
                         CIP

ISBN 0-8118-0434-8 (hardcover)

ISBN 0-8118-0650-2 (paperback)

Printed in Hong Kong.

Distributed in Canada by

Raincoast Books

112 East Third Avenue

Vancouver, BC V5T 1C8

10 9 8 7 6 5 4 3 2 1

Chronicle Books

275 Fifth Street

San Francisco, CA 94103

CONTENTS

ACKNOWLEDGMENTS

Making this book was a labor of love, accomplished only with the creativity and generosity of many people. Our thanks to the following: Nion McEvoy, Charlotte Stone, Michael Carabetta, and the staff at Chronicle Books for their lasting patience and support. • Warmest thanks to friend and visonary designer Jennifer Morla whose talents and energy provided inspiration for this book from day one. • Our heartfelt appreciation to Carolyn Miller for bringing her love of words and coffee and blending them here. • We are deeply grateful to Sandra Cook for her grace, graciousness, and great food. • For providing us with wonderful San Francisco locations, we would like to express appreciation to our local cafés: South Park Café, Caffè Centro, Farley's, Café Claude, Café Tiramisú, Universal Café, and Stars Café, and in Seattle, Café Septieme and Penny U. • For the use of their beautiful things we would like to thank the following shops: Fillamento, Sue Fisher King, and M. Dorain. • Special thanks to Sharrie Brooks at Morla Design. • Thanks also for the support and behind-the-scenes work of Katrine Naleid, Wendi Nordeck, and Vicki Russel-Roberts. • And to the following for providing us with on-going support and generosity, our special thanks to: Jim Stockton, Kathleen Petzke, Karen Tucker, Galen Blakenship, Alice Rogers, Dianne Bertram, Louise Fili, Robert Voorhees, Debra Jones, David Barich, Dana Zavack, Steven Barclay, Emily Luchetti, and Nilus de Matran.

Karl Petzke & Sara Slavin

For their love: Alfred & Georgiann Petzke, my sibling clan, and my friend T.E.H. *K.P.*

With love to Lillian Moss, Sybil Slavin, Kate Slavin, and Mark Steisel. *S.S.*

IT WAS A PLEASANT CAFÉ, WARM AND CLEAN AND FRIENDLY, AND I HUNG UP MY OLD WATER-PROOF ON THE COAT RACK TO DRY AND PUT MY WORN AND WEATHERED FELT HAT ON THE RACK ABOVE THE BENCH AND ORDERED A *CAFÉ AU LAIT*. THE WAITER BROUGHT IT AND I TOOK OUT A NOTEBOOK FROM THE POCKET OF THE COAT AND A PENCIL AND STARTED TO WRITE.

ERNEST HEMINGWAY, *A MOVEABLE FEAST*

Some people don't like espresso. They think it's too strong, too dark. They think espresso is too rich and too bitter, and they don't want to drink coffee out of little cups. But people who don't like espresso almost always like espresso drinks—cappuccino, caffè latte, caffè mocha—in which the intensity of espresso is soothed by hot steamed milk...maybe sweetened with sugar and topped with chocolate or spice.

We like it all: a latte or cappuccino in the morning to wake us up and keep us awake until noon; a demitasse of espresso or a cup of double espresso after lunch to power us through the afternoon; an espresso or an espresso drink mid-afternoon as a break in our day; a stop in a café at the end of the afternoon, to read or write or just sit; an espresso after dinner as the finishing touch to a good meal; a macchiato or a mocha with friends at a coffeehouse in the evening, or after a movie or a play, with something sweet.

Espresso is an acquired taste, but like all acquired tastes, it creates an appetite that no other object or substance of desire can satisfy. For us, espresso is the essence of coffee, that Mediterranean drink, as perfume is the essence of flowers and brandy the essence of wine. It signifies all that is good about the regions of the sun: the love of life, the love of words and images and ideas, the sweetness of doing nothing, the art of inhabiting the earth.

❚

From the beginning, coffee was prized for its stimulating effects; centuries before it became a beverage, the green beans were ground, mixed with fat, and eaten by the Africans as a mild stimulant. Coffee

(continued on page 14)

THE ITALIANS KNOW THAT
COUNTRY IS . . . IMBUED
KNOW THAT THERE IS
DISTINGUISH OR TO
SMILE ON THE FACE OF
DONATELLO'S SAN GIOR-
WORKS OF ART, THE
HAPPY' AND OF MAKING
AN ART WHICH EMBRACES
OTHERS IN ITALY, THE
ING, BUT WHICH CAN
MASTERED, THE ART OF

EVERYTHING IN THEIR
WITH THEIR SPIRIT. THEY
NO NEED, REALLY, TO
CHOOSE BETWEEN THE
A *CAMERIERE* AND
GIO.... THEY ARE ALL
'GREAT ART OF BEING
OTHER PEOPLE HAPPY,
AND INSPIRES ALL
ONLY ART WORTH LEARN-
NEVER BE REALLY
INHABITING THE EARTH.

LUIGI BARZINI, *THE ITALIANS*

trees first grew wild in the high mountain rain forests of Ethiopia; because they need both heat and a fair amount of water, they will grow only in the more temperate areas of the tropics.

By the sixth century A.D., coffee trees were being cultivated in what is today the country of Yemen, on the Arabian peninsula, where the raw husks of coffee cherries and their seeds were crushed and used to make a kind of tea. No one knows who first accidentally dropped the green beans into the fire and witnessed their alchemical change into aromatic roasted beans, but the first coffee was probably made from grinding the roasted beans in a mortar, stirring the grounds into boiling water, and repeatedly heating this mixture to a boil over a flame to make the thick, grainy drink that we now call Turkish coffee.

Brewed coffee was first reserved exclusively for the medical profession and the priesthood; medical men considered it a digestive, and Islamic priests used it as a holy drink to keep them awake through long nights of religious practice. But coffee quickly found its way into the marketplace—for of course it was impossible to ignore the aroma of fresh coffee floating on the desert air—and soon coffeehouses were common in the souks and the bazaars. Today that elemental drink has been transformed through a modern alchemy into the small cups of espresso made daily in coffeehouses around the world, but for us, coffee still retains the aura of its exotic past.

WHEN YOU BRING A BROWN
PAPER BAG OF COFFEE
HOME FROM THE MARKET,
THE STRONG FRAGRANCE
OF DARK-ROASTED BEANS
ACCOMPANIES YOU EVERY-
WHERE YOU GO, PERFUM-
ING THE AIR AROUND YOU
WITH THE PROMISE OF
THE RICH BREW TO COME.

The similarity of espresso to other good-quality coffees starts and ends with the arabica coffee bean, because *espresso* means, first of all, a certain blend of coffee beans, a blend that depends on the coffee roaster's individual taste. *Espresso* also means a color of roasted beans, specifically a dark roast, though the degree of darkness also depends on the roaster's preference. After roasting, the beans are finely ground into an espresso grind, which may vary slightly depending on the kind of espresso machine being used. The espresso grind then must be brewed by the espresso method, which is different from other brewing methods in that it uses pressure to force water through the coffee grounds, rather than allowing gravity to draw water through the grounds. The drink that results from all these fine particulars is—if the espresso maker has followed all the right-steps—the hot, black, lightly textured, fine-foam-covered, deeply flavored drink that we call espresso.

The first commercial espresso machines were manufactured in Italy in 1903, and the drink soon became the quintessential coffee-house beverage. Today it has spread to other countries and is no longer an exclusively urban drink—espresso is found everywhere, in small towns and villages and even on some country roads, and in any kitchen with an espresso maker and a jar of dark-roast beans.

❚

Almost all the taste of coffee comes from its aroma, and it's the aroma that reaches our senses first: wafting out of the kitchen when someone else is already up and has started the coffee; bursting out of the brown paper bag or canister when we open it to grind the day's first coffee beans; layering the air of city streets.

Much of the pleasure of espresso is in its immediate sensual appeal. Everything about espresso is *more so:* more aroma, more taste, more body. It is coffee intensified, and the aroma appeals to us first on a primitive, instinctual level. The process of making individual cups on the spot is another element of the ritual pleasure of this drink: first the wait, then the taste of the dense hot liquid with its cover of *crema,* the fine cinnamon-colored foam that marks a perfect cup of espresso.

❚

Coffee beans begin as flowers— waxy, white, strongly perfumed flowers that cover the branches of coffee trees and send their scent over acres of plantation. The "bean" itself is one of the two seeds inside the berry that develops from each flower. First green, then yellow, when ripe the berry—called a cherry—turns a bright carmine red. The coffee we drink is made from the dried and roasted seeds of these ripe berries. Before they are roasted, "green" coffee beans are a light olive tan, then they dry to a pale yellow-orange. Of the different roasting methods, espresso roast is one of the darkest, turning each bean to the color of bitter chocolate or almost black, and shining with an aromatic oil that has been transmuted from a flower's heavy perfume.

❚

Although most people assume espresso to be as strong in caffeine as it is in flavor and aroma, it contains less than one half to one third of the caffeine in a cup of coffee brewed from robusta beans, the cheaper coffee beans used for

canned coffee. Arabica beans, the high-quality beans used for espresso, have less caffeine. The dark-roast process, which concentrates the flavor of the beans used to make an espresso blend, also has the effect of burning off some of their caffeine content, so that the darker the roast, the lower the caffeine. Espresso roasting adds the hint of an almost-burned odor, what one roaster describes as *caramelly:* a slightly smoky flavor and smell, a dusky quality that satisfies some inner human need for intense taste and fragrance.

❡

Coffee entered Europe through the port of Venice at the end of the sixteenth century, during the late Renaissance. The first European coffee shops were in Venice, and from there the custom of coffee drinking spread throughout the continent. The first espresso machine prototype was invented by a Frenchman, and a larger version, developed in 1843, was the hit of the Paris Exposition in 1855. Steam was the first great power source of the industrial age, used to move ships on the ocean and trains on land. The espresso machine was a true child of the modern era, for it used the same power source. These early machines, like the small countertop machines sold for home use today, heated water to a boil, causing steam to build up in the top of the tall machine. The operator then opened a valve set below the level of the water, and the pressure caused by the built-up steam forced the hot water down the valve and through the packed, finely ground espresso.

AFTER ALL, COFFEE IS BITTER, A FLAVOR FROM THE FORBIDDEN AND DANGEROUS REALM.

DIANE ACKERMAN, *A NATURAL HISTORY OF THE S*

It was the Italians who manufactured the first commercial espresso machines at the turn of the century in Milan, and it was the fine Italian hand that fashioned the machines into tall, baroque, operatic marvels of gleaming brass and copper, emblems of a new century topped with the imperial eagle. In the thirties, Francesco Illy created an espresso machine that forced compressed air, rather than steam, through the grounds, which allowed more control over the temperature level.

The spring-powered piston-lever machine was invented by another Italian, Achille Gaggia, in 1945. Instead of opening a valve, the espresso maker pulled on a long handle, which compressed a spring-loaded piston and forced hot water through the grounds with much more pressure than did the steam method. Because these machines no longer depended on steam to gather above the hot water, they no longer needed to be tall and narrow, and so they lost their knobs and handles and levers and became horizontal and streamlined. That version of the espresso machine has evolved into a hydraulic-pump machine operated by a pushbutton or a lever, although many café owners still prefer piston-lever machines, as they give the espresso maker more control over the brewing process.

It's the process of forcing hot water through the coffee grounds under high pressure that makes espresso such good coffee. The espresso brewing method forces the maximum amount of flavor and body out of the grind in the shortest amount of time—yielding a cup of coffee that is served immediately, before it has any chance to grow stale and bitter.

The best espresso machines are the large, expensive ones that use high pressure, although at home most people use small counter machines, or stovetop espresso makers such as the classic hourglass-shaped Moka or the Atomic, an endearing machine with convoluted curves and a vaguely anatomical form that give it the appearance of a small Henry Moore sculpture. Many of the best espresso machines are still made by Italian companies, and espresso seems to be an elementally *Italian* drink expressive of some essential part of the Italian nature: dramatic, intense, stimulating, alive.

mo**R**ning

...THE FIRE WAS ALREADY BLAZING, FED WITH DRY WOOD. THE MILK WAS BOILING ON THE BLUE-TILED CHARCOAL STOVE. NEARBY, A BAR OF CHOCOLATE WAS MELTING IN A LITTLE WATER FOR MY BREAKFAST, AND, SEATED SQUARELY IN HER CANE ARMCHAIR, MY MOTHER WAS GRINDING THE FRAGRANT COFFEE, WHICH SHE ROASTED HERSELF.

COLETTE, *LA MAISON DE CLAUDINE*

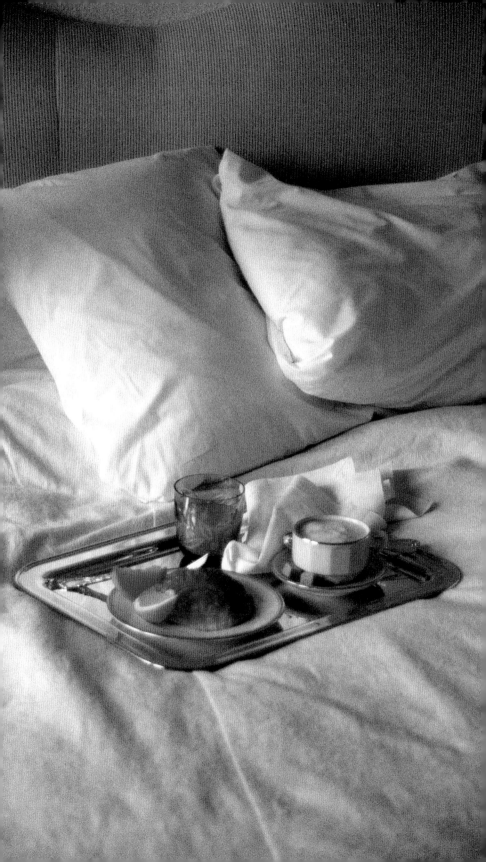

They arrived late at night in a city they had never seen. It was hard to tell much from the windows of the taxi, but although everything about the lobby of the small hotel was unquestionably foreign, arriving there seemed oddly like coming home. They were too tired even to unpack, so they crawled into the high bed and fell asleep under a thick quilt. In the middle of the night he woke up to hear the sound of people singing as they walked by under the windows, and he got up and opened the shutters slightly. Groups of people were strolling by, laughing and talking, coming home very late from dinner. He woke a second time, much later, to hear the sound of rain falling lightly in the street.

The next morning they opened their eyes to find that the room already was filled with barred light coming in through the shutters. A bowl of white flowers was on a table next to the bed, and they could smell the closed, secret smell of the blossoms. She called for room service, speaking very slowly and clearly in her newly acquired language, then came back to bed. Both of them had drifted back to sleep by the time the knock came on the door. A young boy who seemed to have stepped out of a Renaissance painting came in carrying a tray of pastries and preserves...fresh juice and a pot of strong, hot coffee. They ate breakfast sitting up in bed, listening to the sounds of scooters and small cars and people calling out to one another on the other side of the shutters.

They had nothing to do for days— nothing except to be with each other, to read and write, to explore the city, to sit outside little trattorias in the sun. They both got out of bed and walked over to the high windows and out onto the small balcony. In the narrow, winding stone-paved street, the morning light made an intricate pattern of sun and shade on the cornices and lintels and pilasters of ancient, honey-colored limestone buildings. The air had a fragrance that they couldn't quite identify, but after standing there a minute or two in the sunlight, they decided that it was a mixture of lemons, jasmine, and espresso.

❏

The Italian word *espresso* means "express," which is usually defined as "fast" and thought to owe its origin to the speed with which espresso is made, a description of the sudden emergence of inky espresso spurting out of an espresso machine. But of course *express* also refers to an object or substance that has been "pressed out," as espresso is pressed by force out of the mixture of coffee grounds and hot water, and *expressly* means "particularly," as in a cup of espresso made expressly for one person.

❏

The Capuchin order—named after the *cappuccio*, or hood, of the order's habit—has had monasteries in Italy for hundreds of years, and the people of Rome are most familiar with the sight of Capuchin monks in their drab-colored robes. When espresso was invented around the turn of the century, it didn't take

(continued on page 49)

ESPRESSO

One shot (about 1-1/2 ounces, or 3 tablespoons) of espresso served in a 2-1/2-ounce cup. In Italy, this is simply called *un caffè* (its full name is *caffè espresso*) and is meant to be consumed in one swallow as a kind of punctuation point after meals and throughout the day.

CAFFÈ MACCHIATO

Espresso served in an espresso cup but "marked" with a dollop of foamed milk.

CAFFÈ LATTE

A double shot of espresso in a tall glass filled with steamed milk (about 5 ounces) and topped with little or no foam.

CAPPUCCINO

Usually one third espresso, one third steamed milk, and one third foam, served in a 6-ounce ceramic cup. Italian variations are *cappuccino senza fiuma* (without foamed milk), *cappuccino chiaro* ("light" cappuccino with less espresso and more steamed milk), and *cappuccino scuro* ("dark" cappuccino with more espresso and less milk).

ESPRESSO SYRUP

We like this spicy, deep-flavored syrup on waffles, pancakes, and French toast, but it's just as good over vanilla, chocolate, or hazelnut gelato. It will keep for weeks in a tightly closed jar in the refrigerator.

3/4 cup sugar

1/4 cup water

1/2 cup brewed espresso

2 teaspoons grated orange zest

1 teaspoon ground cinnamon

In a small, heavy saucepan, combine the sugar and water over medium heat, stirring until the sugar dissolves. Bring the mixture to a boil and cook for 3 to 4 minutes. Remove the pan from the heat, stir, and let the mixture cool for 1 minute. Stir in the espresso, orange zest, and cinnamon. Pour the syrup into a jar and let sit for at least 30 minutes before using.

Makes about 1 cup.

ON SATURDAY MORNINGS I WOULD WALK TO THE FLAVOR CUP OR PORTO RICO IMPORTING COFFEE STORE TO GET MY COFFEE. OFTEN IT WAS FRESHLY ROASTED AND THE BEANS WERE STILL WARM. COFFEE WAS MY NECTAR AND MY AMBROSIA: I WAS VERY CAREFUL ABOUT IT. I DE-CANTED MY BEANS INTO GLASS... AND I GROUND THEM IN LITTLE BATCHES IN MY GRINDER.

LAURIE COLWIN, *HOME COOKING*

BISCOTTI WITH TOASTED ESPRESSO BEANS

A double hit of espresso: biscotti made with both toasted espresso beans and brewed espresso, to dunk in your morning or afternoon cup. These lightly sweet cookies will keep a long time in a tightly closed tin and are even better a day or so after baking.

1-1/4 cups (6 ounces) almonds

6 tablespoons espresso beans

2-1/2 cups unbleached
   all-purpose flour

2 teaspoons baking powder

1 teaspoon salt

1/2 cup (1 stick) chilled unsalted
   butter, cut into small pieces

1 cup sugar

3 eggs, lightly beaten

1/4 cup brewed espresso

Ground cinnamon or cocoa for
   dusting

Preheat an oven to 350°F. Spread the almonds and espresso beans on 2 separate baking sheets and place in the oven for 8 to 10 minutes, or until lightly toasted. Remove the nuts and espresso beans from the oven and leave the oven on.

Using a large knife, a blender, or a food processor, coarsely chop 3 tablespoons of the espresso beans. Finely chop the almonds in a blender or food processor. In a coffee grinder, finely grind the remaining 3 tablespoons espresso beans.

In a large bowl, combine the flour, baking powder, and salt. With a pastry blender or 2 knives, cut in the butter until it resembles coarse meal. Add the nuts, both the ground and the chopped espresso beans, sugar, eggs, and brewed espresso. Mix well.

On a lightly floured board, knead the dough for 2 minutes and divide it into 2 pieces. Shape each piece into a thin roll about 2 inches in diameter and dust each roll with cinnamon or cocoa. Place on greased baking sheets and bake for 25 minutes, or until lightly browned.

Using a serrated knife, cut each roll into 1-1/2-inch crosswise slices on the diagonal. Lay the slices on their sides and bake another 8 to 10 minutes on each side, or until just lightly golden. Let cool on racks and store in a tightly closed tin. Makes about 48 biscotti.

ESPRESSO-HAZELNUT SCONES

Hazelnuts, brown sugar, and brewed and ground espresso make flavorful scones to serve for a morning treat. Serve warm or at room temperature.

1-1/4 cups (6 ounces) hazelnuts

1-1/2 tablespoons espresso beans

1/3 cup milk

1/3 cup brewed espresso

2-1/2 cups unbleached

all-purpose flour

1 tablespoon baking powder

1/2 teaspoon salt

8 tablespoons cold unsalted

butter

1/3 cup packed brown sugar

Preheat an oven to 350°F. Place the hazelnuts and espresso beans in separate shallow baking pans and place them in the oven for 8 to 10 minutes, or until lightly toasted. Wrap the nuts in a clean dish towel and let cool. Rub the nuts between the cloth or your hands to remove the dark brown skins. Chop the nuts coarsely by hand or in a blender or food processor; grind the espresso beans very finely in a coffee grinder.

Turn the oven up to 400°F. In a small bowl, combine the milk and brewed espresso. Add the ground espresso beans and set aside. In a large bowl, thoroughly mix the flour, baking powder, and salt. Cut in the butter with a pastry blender or 2 knives until the mixture resembles coarse meal.

Add the hazelnuts and brown sugar, mixing lightly just to blend. Add the espresso mixture and stir with a wooden spoon until a soft dough forms. Place the dough on a lightly floured board, knead into a ball, and form into a 7-inch round. Cut the round into 6 to 8 wedges and place them slightly apart on an ungreased baking sheet. Bake for 20 to 25 minutes, or until a toothpick inserted in the center of a scone comes out clean. Let cool slightly on a wire rack. Makes 6 to 8 large scones.

CAFFÈ MOCHA

About one third espresso, one third steamed milk, and one third cocoa served in a tall glass; sometimes made with 1 to 2 tablespoons of chocolate syrup and more milk.

CAFÉ AU LAIT

The real thing is made with equal parts drip-brewed French roast coffee and heated milk poured simultaneously into a café au lait bowl, but many coffeehouses make it with espresso and steamed milk.

CAFFÈ RISTRETTO

"Restricted" espresso is for the truly dedicated espresso-lover; it uses only 1 ounce of water and the same amount of coffee grounds to make the strongest and most concentrated of espressos.

CAFFÈ CORRETTO

Espresso "corrected" by being laced with a shot of brandy or liqueur.

long for some clever espresso maker to realize that the steam produced by the espresso machine also could be used to heat milk to add to the espresso—and as a great bonus, the steamed milk was covered with a billowing cloud of foam. Adding one part steamed milk to one part espresso and topping it with one part foam makes a drink that, for Romans, is best described as being the same muddy brown as the robes of the Capuchin brothers: *cappuccino*, or "little Capuchin."

❡

In San Francisco, the sharp, acrid smell of roasting coffee ascends every day in clouds of vapor over North Beach, where it drifts across the grass of Washington Square Park in front of the church of Saints Peter and Paul, past the old men sitting on the park benches, and over the bakeries with their trays of focaccia and country loaves and *panini*, and by the coffee-houses where people sit drinking cappuccino and caffè latte, part of the enduring ceremony of morning in the city.

❡

In Rome, beautifully dressed Italians are drinking their morning coffee on the run, standing at the counters of little espresso bars, drinking cappuccino out of small dark brown china cups and eating flaky *cornetti*. Parisian blue-collar workers are drinking espresso and eating French bread at truck stops and in smoky old bars in the Marais, and office workers are stopping in cafés for a bowl of café au lait to cradle in their hands, and a croissant with butter and jam. In American cities, people who have rushed to get to work are standing in line to order muffins or scones and paper cups of cappuccino or latte.

Monday morning, and you're already late to work. The bus was twenty minutes late, and it will take you a good five minutes to walk from the bus stop through the crowded downtown streets. You didn't bring an umbrella since the weather report didn't mention rain, but it is definitely raining on the new shoes you paid too much for, and on your hair, which is slowly collapsing into clumps.

No time today for either breakfast or coffee, but everybody on the street seems to be carrying a white paper cup and drinking out of the plastic lid—a few have brought their own ceramic cups to the take-out window and are carefully carrying them down the street so they won't lose any foam. People are driving by holding a commuter cup in one hand and trying to steer with the other. Even the bike messengers are cutting across the traffic lanes and in front of cars at a perilous speed while balancing a take-out cup on a handlebar.

The people who aren't carrying coffee are lined up to buy it at espresso carts and bars along the street, like this one with a line of ten people coming out the door. If you stop now, you'll be at least twenty minutes late for work by the time you get your coffee and make it to the office—and after all, there is coffee there, okay coffee made in an automatic drip machine. But of course that's not the same as espresso—it just doesn't have the same good, strong taste, doesn't really start the day off quite the same way— besides, you're hungry, and from the street you can see a pyramid of fresh whole-wheat banana muffins and sticky buns and thick slices of apple-walnut bread, and cranberry scones, like the one that woman is just carrying out of the shop.

rituals

MY FIFTIETH YEAR HAD
COME AND GONE, / I
SAT, A SOLITARY MAN, /
IN A CROWDED LONDON
SHOP, / AN OPEN BOOK
AND EMPTY CUP / ON
THE MARBLE TABLE-TOP.
WHILE ON THE SHOP AND
STREET I GAZED / MY
BODY OF A SUDDEN
BLAZED; / AND TWENTY
MINUTES MORE OR LESS /
IT SEEMED, SO GREAT MY
HAPPINESS, / THAT I
WAS BLESSÈD AND COULD
BLESS.

W. B. YEATS, FROM "VACILLATION"

Cafés and coffeehouses are more than just way stations: they are both havens from the workplace and substitutes for it. Hemingway, Simone de Beauvoir, Sartre, and multitudes of other writers, both acclaimed and unknown, have written novels, treatises, and poems in cafés with a cup of coffee at their elbow. Since the time of the Renaissance, scientists, thinkers, and revolutionaries of all kinds have found their home in clean, well-lighted coffeehouses, and coffee has been a working companion, an assistant to the muse, and both an essential and a ritual element in the act of creation.

TOASTED ESPRESSO NUTS

Warm and spicy, these mixed nuts are a good hors d'oeuvre to serve with vodka or chilled white wine.

1 cup (5 ounces) almonds or mixed raw nuts
1 tablespoon vegetable oil
1 teaspoon finely ground espresso
1 teaspoon garlic powder
1 teaspoon salt
1 teaspoon ground nutmeg
Pinch of cayenne pepper

Preheat an oven to 350°F. In a small bowl, toss the nuts in the oil, then place them on a baking sheet. Place in the oven for 8 to 10 minutes, or until lightly toasted. In a medium bowl, combine all of the remaining ingredients and toss the nuts in this mixture until they are lightly coated. Return the nuts to the baking sheet and toast for 2 more minutes. Serve warm or at room temperature.

Makes about 1 cup.

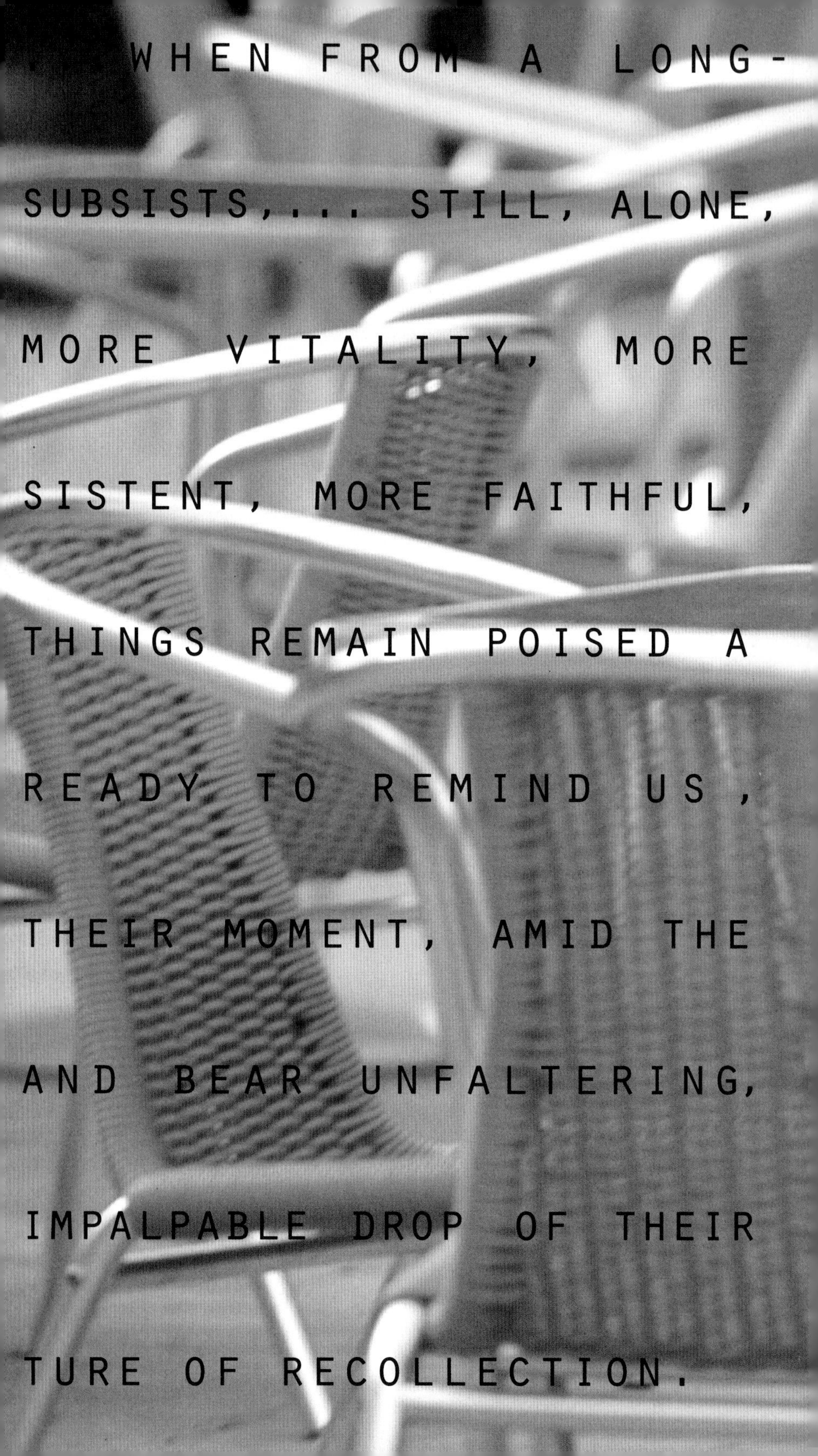

WHEN FROM A LONG-

SUBSISTS,... STILL, ALONE,

MORE VITALITY, MORE

SISTENT, MORE FAITHFUL,

THINGS REMAIN POISED A

READY TO REMIND US,

THEIR MOMENT, AMID THE

AND BEAR UNFALTERING,

IMPALPABLE DROP OF THEIR

TURE OF RECOLLECTION.

DISTANT PAST NOTHING

MORE FRAGILE, BUT WITH

UNSUBSTANTIAL, MORE PER-

THE SMELL AND TASTE OF

LONG TIME, LIKE SOULS,

WAITING AND HOPING FOR

RUINS OF ALL THE REST;

IN THE TINY AND ALMOST

ESSENCE, THE VAST STRUC-

MARCEL PROUST, SWANN'S WAY

ESPRESSO SORBETTO

A simple sweet that is low in calories and refreshing by itself or at the end of a meal.

1-1/2 cups brewed espresso

4 sugar cubes

2 cups low-fat milk

Pour the espresso into an ice cube tray and freeze until solid. Place the frozen espresso and the remaining ingredients in a blender or food processor and blend for 3 minutes, or until smooth. Or, make the sorbetto in an ice cream maker, following the manufacturer's instructions. Serve in frosted glasses. Serves 4 to 6.

ICED ESPRESSO

To coffee-lovers, iced coffee drinks are like another room in heaven: a whole new category of ways to enjoy espresso. There's something deeply pleasing about the contrast of being surrounded by warm air while drinking chilled, strong, sweet coffee; nothing is quite as satisfying on a hot afternoon or a warm summer night as sitting at a café table with a tall beaded glass of iced cappuccino or espresso.

One shot of espresso and one shot of milk poured over ice. In Italy this is called *caffè con ghiaccio e latte*.

The Fifties: Ike was in the White House, and the country was deep in conformity and conservatism. But in the bars and coffeehouses of San Francisco, a small group of writers were looking at life through different eyes. The Beat Generation was based in the inexpensive apartments of North Beach and fueled by cheap red wine and strong dark coffee. Coffeehouses like the Coffee Gallery and the Co-existence Bagel Shop provided table space and espresso for such writers as Allen Ginsberg, Lawrence Ferlinghetti, Jack Kerouac, Gary Snyder, and Bob Kaufman. Old photographs show them all looking impossibly young, crowded together in smoky spaces, not knowing ... or perhaps knowing ... that their world of berets and sunglasses and mountain red and cigarettes and old wooden tables holding messily handwritten manuscripts would someday be part of literary history.

CHOCOLATE ESPRESSO BEANS

These little after-dinner treats are easy to make and hard to stop eating. Serve with espresso and gelato.

1 cup espresso beans

4 ounces milk chocolate

3 tablespoons cocoa

Preheat an oven to 350°F. Place the espresso beans on a baking sheet and toast for 8 to 10 minutes. Let cool. Melt the chocolate in a double boiler over barely simmering water until smooth and creamy. Drop in the espresso beans and stir until the beans are coated. Remove the beans with a slotted spoon and allow the excess chocolate to drip off. Place the beans on waxed paper, separating them so they do not stick together.

When the coated beans are cool but the chocolate is still pliable, roll the beans in your hands to form round balls. Roll each ball in cocoa and set aside until the chocolate coating has set completely. Makes about 1-1/2 cups.

ESPRESSO BRITTLE

This special brittle made with cracked toasted espresso beans is a good gift to make for the holidays. Espresso brittle will keep for up to a week in a tightly closed tin.

1/3 cup espresso beans

1-1/2 cups sugar

3/4 cup light corn syrup

1/2 cup water

3 tablespoons unsalted butter, cut into pieces

Preheat an oven to 350°F. Place the espresso beans on a baking sheet and toast them for 8 to 10 minutes. Let cool, then crack them by placing them in a plastic bag and hitting them with a mallet. Cover 10- by 15-inch jelly roll pan in aluminum foil and lightly oil the foil. Spread the cracked espresso beans evenly over the foil.

In a medium-sized, heavy saucepan, combine the sugar, syrup, and water and bring the mixture to a boil, stirring until the sugar dissolves. Continue to boil until the liquid becomes amber in color. Remove from heat, stir in the butter, and pour the mixture evenly over the beans. Spread the mixture evenly while still warm. Let cool, then break into irregular pieces. Makes about 1 pound.

POACHED FIGS WITH ESPRESSO

An ambrosial dish that combines espresso, fresh raspberries, and Cabernet Sauvignon—a perfect dessert for a late-summer evening.

8 fresh figs

1/2 cup water

1/4 cup brewed espresso

1/2 cup fresh raspberries

1/4 cup Cabernet Sauvignon

3 strips lemon zest

2 teaspoons sugar

3 or 4 whole cloves

Slice the figs in half lengthwise and set aside. In a medium saucepan, combine all the remaining ingredients. Simmer over medium-low heat for 8 minutes, or until the sugar is dissolved, stirring occasionally. Place the figs in the pan and simmer for 3 minutes. Divide the figs between 4 shallow bowls and pour the warm sauce over them. Serve at once.

Serves 4.

Part of the appeal of coffee is that it is a drink that marks the transitions in our day: the transition from sleeping to waking, from work to rest, from day to night. It marks the end of meals and the end of solitude, and accompanies us through the day like a talisman of both change and continuity.

❡

Rumi was a thirteenth-century Sufi who wrote radiant poems of spiritual longing and mystical transformation. He was also the founder of the order of the whirling dervishes. Before coffee was adopted by the masses, it was the ritual drink of priests and acolytes, who used it as an aid to meditation and prayer. We like to think of Rumi whirling and whirling for hours in his sky blue Sufi robes, transported to another reality by constant movement and many tiny cups of ceremonially brewed coffee, the patron dervish of all future coffeehouse poets.

Existentialism, feminism, and the modern novel were all partly shaped in the cafés of Paris. Jean-Paul Sartre and Simone de Beauvoir first wrote in Le Dôme until it was taken over by German soldiers in 1940, at which time they moved to Café de Flore.

❡

One of the oldest European coffeehouses, Caffè Greco in Rome was founded sometime before 1750. A popular stop on the Grand Tour, it has hosted some of the greatest writers and musicians of Western civilization. Caffè Greco is located on Via Condotti at the foot of the Spanish Steps.

café
sOciety

THE WINE IMPROVES ...
THE CANDLES BEGIN
TO FLICKER. THERE IS
BITTER BLACK COFFEE,
SITTING CARELESSLY
BESIDE THE LAST BITS
OF CHEESE, THE LAST
FRECKLED CRUMBS OF
BREAD UPON THE CLOTH.

M.F.K. FISHER, FROM "AN ALPHABET FOR GOURMETS"

Napoleon once called St. Mark's Square in Venice the living room of Europe, but that was a typically grandiose Napoleonic statement. In a continent of cities filled with small, dark, and cold apartments with minimal kitchen facilities, the real living rooms of Europe, as social scientists have pointed out, were the cafés and coffeehouses that sprang up in profusion once coffee was introduced there.

Coffee has been referred to as the drink of democracy, for cafés and coffeehouses were the first public places in Europe where people of all classes and both sexes mingled freely. It was also the first nonalcoholic drink to gain public acceptance. Beer and wine, which were consumed in quantity throughout the Continent, released the inhibitions and deadened the mind, but coffee had just the opposite effect: It stimulated the brain and made one sober and aware.

In this new atmosphere of freedom of assembly and of thought, people began to see the possibility of new ways of being in the world. And almost from the beginning, the established powers understood that the lure of coffee and the public interchange it fostered posed a danger to their authority.

(continued on page 85)

SAUTÉED GRAPES WITH RED WINE AND ESPRESSO

A beautiful combination of colors and tastes, this elegant dish can serve as a side dish for an Italian meal of roast meat or poultry, or as a light dessert with cheese, biscotti, or polenta cake.

1 tablespoon olive oil

1/2 shallot, minced

2 cups mixed grapes

1/4 cup brewed espresso

1/2 cup dry red wine

3 cinnamon sticks

1 tablespoon honey

1/2 tablespoon balsamic vinegar

1/2 tablespoon unsalted butter

Heat the olive oil in a medium sauté pan. Add the shallot and sauté until translucent, about 2 minutes. Add the grapes and sauté for 1 minute. Add the espresso, red wine, cinnamon sticks, and honey. Stir for 2 minutes and remove from heat. Add the vinegar and butter to the pan and stir until the butter melts. Serve warm.

Serves 2 to 4 as a side dish.

CHOCOLATE-ESPRESSO TORTE

Chocolate and espresso are one of the best of all food combinations. Here they give smoothness and depth to a rich, dense torte.

2 tablespoons hazelnuts or almonds
2 tablespoons espresso beans
16 ounces semisweet chocolate
1 cup (2 sticks) unsalted butter
9 eggs, separated
1 cup granulated sugar
1/4 cup brewed espresso
Sifted powdered sugar or cocoa for dusting

Preheat the oven to 350°F. Butter a 10-inch springform pan. Line the bottom with buttered waxed paper and dust the pan with cocoa or finely ground espresso.

Place the nuts and espresso beans in separate shallow baking pans and place them in the oven for 8 to 10 minutes, or until lightly toasted. If using hazelnuts, wrap them in a clean dish towel and let cool, then rub them between the cloth or your hands to remove the dark brown skins. Grind the nuts in a blender or food processor and finely grind the espresso beans in a coffee grinder.

In a heavy saucepan over very low heat, melt the chocolate and butter together. Stir in the ground espresso beans and nuts; pour into a bowl to cool. In a large bowl, beat the yolks for about 1 minute. Slowly add the sugar and continue beating until thick and pale. Add the brewed espresso to the yolk mixture, then add the cooled chocolate mixture and blend thoroughly.

In another large bowl, beat the egg whites until soft peaks form. Pour the chocolate and yolk mixture into the egg whites and fold gently until completely blended. Pour the batter into the prepared pan and bake for 40 to 45 minutes, or until the edges begin to pull away from the sides of the pan.

Let the torte cool on a rack for 30 minutes. Run a knife around the edges of the cake to loosen it, then remove the sides of the pan. Run a long narrow knife under the waxed paper to remove the bottom of the pan. Invert the torte, remove the paper, and place the torte on a serving plate. Dust with powdered sugar or cocoa to serve. Makes one 10-inch torte.

GLAZED APPLES WITH ESPRESSO-CREAM SAUCE

Allspice, honey, espresso, and cream make a smooth, warm sauce to serve over golden-brown baked apples.

4 Granny Smith apples, peeled but uncored

1/4 cup apple juice

1/4 cup honey

3 tablespoons unsalted butter

1 teaspoon ground allspice

1/4 cup brewed espresso

3 tablespoons heavy (whipping) cream

Preheat an oven to 350°F. Place the peeled apples in a shallow baking dish. In a small saucepan, combine the apple juice, honey, butter, allspice, and espresso. Heat until the butter melts, stirring occasionally. Pour the mixture over the apples and bake them for 50 minutes, basting them with the liquid in the baking dish every 10 to 15 minutes.

When the apples are tender and glazed, remove them from the baking dish to a serving plate or plates; set aside and keep warm. Mix the cream with the liquid in the baking dish and serve warm over the apples. Serves 4.

CUTTING THE LEMON
THE KNIFE / LEAVES A
LITTLE / CATHEDRAL:
ALCOVES UNGUESSED BY
THE EYE / THAT OPEN
ACIDULOUS GLASS / TO THE
LIGHT; TOPAZES / RIDING
THE DROPLETS, / ALTARS,
AROMATIC FAÇADES.
SO, WHILE THE HAND
HOLDS THE CUT OF THE
LEMON, / HALF A WORLD
ON A TRENCHER, / THE
GOLD OF THE UNIVERSE
WELLS / TO YOUR TOUCH:
A CUP YELLOW / WITH
MIRACLES. . . .

PABLO NERUDA, FROM "A LEMON"

The thousand-year history of coffee is marked by periodic outbreaks of opposition from the political and medical establishments. Government after government banned coffee and coffeehouses completely, tried to restrict its use to the upper classes, or imposed heavy taxes on its use. None of this worked, however; it was too late. The idea of democracy and equality was alive in the land. At about the same time as the first coffeehouses were established in Europe, the first daily newspapers began to be published. Now the common people had access to information, and a forum where they could discuss it openly.

❏

Although it is sometimes called *caffè romano*, no Roman will agree that espresso served with a twist of lemon is a Roman or even an Italian invention. No one knows who first placed a strip of lemon peel on the saucer along with a cup of espresso, but it seems to be a wholly American custom. Some people say that the lemon was originally intended to mask the taste of inferior espresso. Yet to us, a twist of lemon with espresso has become an accepted convention and even a preferred habit, as the bitter perfume of lemon oil seems to complement the strong taste of espresso, adding another aromatic taste of the south to each miniature cup.

ESPRESSO CRÈME BRULÉE

A classic crème brulée with the added
interest of the rich flavor of both brewed
and ground espresso.

2 cups heavy (whipping) cream

1/2 cup milk

1/4 cup granulated sugar

1/2 cup brewed espresso

3 whole eggs

3 egg yolks

1/2 cup brown sugar

**2 tablespoons finely ground
espresso**

Preheat an oven to 300°F. In a medium saucepan, combine the cream, milk, granulated sugar, and brewed espresso. Place over medium heat for 3 to 5 minutes, or until warm; do not let the mixture boil. Remove from heat. In a medium bowl, beat together the eggs and egg yolks. Gradually stir or whisk the beaten eggs into the heated mixture, then cook over medium heat for 3 minutes, stirring constantly.

Pour the mixture into eight 6-ounce custard cups and place the cups in a shallow baking dish. Add water to the dish to halfway up the sides of the cups. Bake for 35 to 45 minutes, or until the custards are set in the center. Remove from the baking dish and let sit for 1 hour.

Preheat a broiler. Sieve brown sugar evenly over the top of each custard. Place under the broiler for 2 or 3 minutes, or until the sugar begins to melt; be careful not to let it burn. Dust the top of each custard lightly with the ground espresso while the brown sugar is still warm. Chill before serving. Serves 8.

ESPRESSO CHEESECAKE WITH A HAZELNUT CRUST

A light ricotta cheesecake with a hint of espresso and a crunchy nut crust.

HAZELNUT CRUST

2-3/4 cups (14 ounces) hazelnuts

1/4 cup (1/2 stick) butter, melted

1/4 cup sugar

FILLING

4 cups (32 ounces) ricotta cheese*

12 ounces cream cheese at room temperature

3 tablespoons flour

4 eggs, lightly beaten

1 cup packed brown sugar

1/2 cup brewed espresso

1 teaspoon vanilla extract or coffee liqueur

*If you are using very fresh ricotta, you may want to place it in a clean dish towel to squeeze out some of the moisture.

To make the crust: Preheat the oven to 350°F. Place the hazelnuts on a baking sheet and toast in the oven for 8 to 10 minutes. Wrap the nuts in a clean dish towel and let cool, then rub them between the cloth or your hands to remove the dark brown skins. In a blender or food processor, grind the hazelnuts; reserve 2 tablespoons of the ground nuts. In a medium bowl, combine the remaining ground hazelnuts, butter, and sugar until well blended. Starting with the sides, press evenly into a 10-inch springform pan to make a thin crust. Place in the freezer to chill for 15 minutes before filling.

To make the filling: Turn up the oven to 375°F. In a large bowl, using an electric mixer, combine the ricotta and cream cheese and mix on low speed until smooth. Sprinkle in the flour, continuing to blend. Beat in half of the eggs until the mixture is smooth, then beat in the remaining eggs. Gradually beat in the sugar, then the espresso and vanilla or liqueur, until smooth.

Pour into the chilled hazelnut crust and bake for 35 minutes, then check every 5 minutes; the cheesecake is done when a 3-inch ridge has set around the edge of the pan and the inside is partially set and trembling slightly in the center. Sprinkle with the reserved ground hazelnuts and let cool to room temperature in a draft-free place, then refrigerate. Wait about 8 hours before covering the cheesecake with plastic wrap. The flavor and texture will reach their peak between 24 and 36 hours. Serves 6 to 8.

DUCK BREAST WITH PRUNES AND ESPRESSO

The rich flavor of duck marries well with an intriguing mixture of port, espresso, prunes, and fresh herbs.

2 tablespoons butter

1 tablespoon olive oil

2 onions, sliced

4 skinned and boned half duck breasts

2 teaspoons dried thyme

1 cup port

1/2 cup brewed espresso

1/2 cup prune juice

12 whole pitted prunes

Salt and freshly ground pepper to taste

1/4 cup chopped fresh parsley

In a large sauté pan or skillet, melt the butter with the olive oil and sauté the onions until golden, about 5 minutes. Place the duck breasts in the skillet with the onions and cook to lightly brown them on both sides. Remove the duck breasts and set aside. Combine all of the remaining ingredients, except the parsley, in the pan and cook uncovered over very low heat for 20 minutes. Return the duck breasts to the skillet and simmer uncovered for 8 to 10 minutes. Slice each breast thinly, place the slices on warm plates, sprinkle with the parsley, and serve with the warm sauce, prunes, and onions. Serves 4.

Born during the Renaissance, café society was the source of many of the changes that formed our modern world. The coffeehouse was where political revolutions in England, France, and Russia were nurtured and planned; as well as where such revolutions in art and literature as dadaism, futurism, surrealism, cubism, and existentialism were formulated and developed; and where such theoretical disciplines as psychoanalysis and modern physics were brought to life.

❡

A single or double espresso or an espresso macchiato is the perfect final touch to a good meal. If you want a little something extra, there's espresso *con panna*, topped with a dollop of whipped cream, or espresso *corretto*: "corrected," or improved, with the addition of a shot of brandy or liqueur. In Italy this is often grappa; other good choices are any coffee liqueur, or Sambuca, the Italian liqueur with a coffee bean in the bottom of the bottle. An Italian specialty called VOV is a zabaglione liqueur available only in a few coffeehouses in this country.

The strong flavor of espresso is used in a variety of desserts, the simplest being frozen diluted and sweetened espresso, or granita. An even easier dessert, which combines two great Italian culinary gifts, is *affogato al caffè:* vanilla gelato with a shot of hot espresso poured over it. Adding a spoonful of coffee liqueur is optional gilding.

The Italians call it *dolce far niente:* "the sweetness of doing nothing." Americans call it "hanging out" or "hanging." The social scientists discuss "flow experience" and the "expanded present." Buddhists try to live in the moment. All these things can be done in cafés: You can disappear into the written word or the world of your imagination. You can notice and experience everything around you. You can wait for something else to happen. You can stop thinking altogether.

RECIPE LIST

Drinks

Café au Lait	46
Caffè Corretto	46
Caffè Latte	37
Caffè Macchiato	37
Caffè Mocha	46
Caffè Ristretto	46
Cappuccino	37
Espresso	37
Iced Espresso	63

Sweets

Biscotti with Toasted Espresso Beans	42
Chocolate Espresso Beans	66
Chocolate-Espresso Torte	81
Espresso Brittle	66
Espresso Cheesecake with a Hazelnut Crust	89
Espresso Crème Brulée	86
Espresso-Hazelnut Scones	45
Espresso Sorbetto	63
Espresso Syrup	38
Glazed Apples with Espresso-Cream Sauce	82
Poached Figs with Espresso	69

Simple Foods Made with Espresso

Duck Breast with Prunes and Espresso	90
Sautéed Grapes with Red Wine and Espresso	78
Toasted Espresso Nuts	58

96